C000230653

Chenies & Chorleywood
In Camera

by Clive Birch FSA FRSA

QUOTES LIMITED *of* BUCKINGHAM

MCMLXXXVIII

Published by Quotes Limited of Buckingham in 1988
and in this second edition in 1989

Typeset in Plantin by
Key Composition of Northampton, England

Pictures Lithographed by
South Midlands Lithoplates Limited, Luton, England

Printed by Busiprint Limited
Buckingham, England

Bound by Cedric Chivers Limited
Bath, England

© Clive Birch 1988 & 1989

All rights reserved. No part of this publication may be reproduced, stored in a retrieval system, or transmitted, in any form or by any means, electronic, mechanical, photocopying, recording or otherwise, without the prior permission of Quotes Limited.

Any copy of this book issued by the Publisher as clothbound or as a paperback is sold subject to the condition that it shall not by way of trade or otherwise, be lent, re-sold, hired out or otherwise circulated without the Publisher's prior consent, in any form of binding or cover other than that in which it is published, and without a similar condition including this condition being imposed on a subsequent purchaser.

ISBN 0 86023 363 4

Acknowledgements

In writing any book, however modest, no author is on his own. There is always a team — informants, advisers, illustrators, kindly critics, and guides to what is what. My thanks for this volume go to Ginnie Jenkins, who gave me advice, told me stories about the past, and lent me her splendid collection of old Chorleywood postcards; to my good friend Colin Seabright of Chesham Bois, who always offers his comprehensive collection whenever I start another book; to Edith Beech of Chorleywood Library, for patience, organising pictures, and providing the facts; to Shelagh Head, of Hertford's central Local Studies Library, for further guidance and access to county-held originals; to Mrs Maling of Chenies, for welcoming me to her home, and sharing her family pictures, her precious memories, and the tales others told her; to her friends in the village, Mrs Leach and Miss Ruston, for putting me straight on matters of fact, and to various sources of old pictures over the months. And of course, as always, I owe more than I can say to my photographic colleague, John Armistead, who has been improving old pictures for me for over 15 years, and taking new ones for over 30.

CB   Author's collection
HCL   Hertfordshire County Library
RM   Mrs R. Maling
CS   Colin Seabright
VJ   Mrs V. Jenkins

The Book of Chesham Clive Birch, Barracuda Books 1974.

The Book of Chorleywood & Chenies George Ray, Barracuda Books 1983

Concise Oxford Dictionary of English Place Names Eilert Ekwall, Oxford (4th edition) 1960

Domesday Book ed John Morris, Phillimore 1978

Early Man in South Buckinghamshire J. F. Head, Wright & Sons 1955

Hertfordshire Gwennah Robinson, Barracuda Books 1978

History & Antiquities of the County of Buckingham George Lipscomb, J. & W. Robins, 1847

History & Topography of Buckinghamshire Sheahan, Longman, 1862

Maps of Bucks Gordon Wyatt, Barracuda Books 1979

Post Office Directory of Northamptonshire, Huntingdonshire, Bedfordshire and Buckinghamshire Kelly & Co., 1864 & 1887 *of Hertfordshire* Kelly & Co., 1869, 1890 & 1937

Development Plan 1951 – Chorleywood Herts County Council

Urban District of Chorleywood Official Guide 1972

Records of Buckinghamshire Bucks Archaeological Society, 1863 to date

Victoria History — Buckinghamshire and *Hertfordshire* ed William Page 1925, reprinted Dawsons of Pall Mall 1904

Yesterday's Town: Chesham Clive Birch & John Armistead, Barracuda Books 1977

Note: This edition has been revised with the help of Elsie Bate, Mr Haynes, Alexandra Fowkes, Dorothy Cooper and Margaret C. Corcoran, to all of whom I am grateful for their time and interest.

Romantics tell of tunnels, from Chenies Manor to Chalfont Road; of how the river Chess christened a town, the ruins of a church upon its banks, and the ancient origins of Charley's Wood. The 'realists' dismiss Chenies as a picturesque village off the road to Watford, and Chorleywood as a soulless railway town. The truth lies elsewhere.

The tunnel is a myth, but there is an underground cul-de-sac in the Manor grounds — believed to be a bolthole for Civil War combatants — and a splendid priest-hole, once concealed within the house itself. The river takes its name from nearby Chesham, and Chorleywood *is* a railway town — with a Roman past.

The Cilternsaetan tribe roamed the area 500 years before Domesday, but the Chess Valley was a wilderness — the 'deserts of Chiltern'. It was not always so. During the Roman occupation, half a millenium before, a string of prosperous Romano-British farms spread along the river valley, from Chorleywood's later site, via Sarratt and Latimer, to Weirhouse Mill and Chesham. The estate across the river from Mount Farm ran to some 450 acres.

In late Saxon times, the farmers returned, not least to Isenhampstede on the river *Isa* or *Isene* — the iron stream. By the 13th century, Isenhampstead Latimers was distinguished from Isenhampstead Chenduit by the name of its lord. Chenies is a 'modern' name, from Cheney or *chene* (French = oak) which comes from *casnetum*, the latin for oak grove. Ralph de Casinetto was said to have joined William the Bastard, in his territorial adventure of 1066.

Ceorla is old English for peasant; the peasant's wood probably meant the manorial waste, or commonland, fit for lower ranks alone. The river itself became the Chess, from the same Saxon root as Chesham — *Caestelshamm*, the stone settlement on the river — after that had been corrupted to Chessum.

By Domesday, Mainou the Breton held something like 500 acres in Chalfont St Giles — most of the later Chenies estate and probably Chorleywood West as well. On the Herts side, Chorleywood was simply an unimportant appendage of Rickmansworth Manor, in the hands of Mother Church, specifically my lord Abbot of St Albans — until Henry Tudor changed the rules, and nationalised the good Lord's lands.

Cheney was certainly important enough to rate a mention in Henry's informal survey, conducted by the King's itinerant reporter, John Leland — and it found itself mapped as well, by Saxton's *Buckingham/Comitatus* in 1573. But John Speed cut it out again in his record of 1610. By 1627 it was back on all the maps. Morden added Latimers (and Flandon) in 1680, but John Ellis was the first to show us Chorley Wood, in his 1766 *Modern Map of Buckinghamshire;* he dropped Chenies. Yet even in the 19th century, Chorleywood was frequently ignored.

It was in 1165 that Isenhampstead was first documented: the estate of one Alexander, ancestor of the 1232 Alexander Cheyne. In 1526 it fell to the Russells, via the marriage bed, and there it stayed for nearly 450 years. They left an indelible mark: the first Earl rebuilt the Manor House, and several surviving cottages date to his tenure. The 19th century Russells virtually rebuilt the place; best remembered was rector Lord Wriothesley Russell, who also raised the schoolhouse. He started the 'model village' reflective of the surging spirit of tenant welfare, which characterised many paternalists of the time, and was seen elsewhere in the Russell domain, principally at Woburn.

And there remains one enduring link between family and place. The Dukes are all laid to rest in their own chapel at St Michael's, Chenies, even in our own times.

In 1862, Chenies was still Isenhampstead Chenies, covered 1,744 acres and housed 469 people. Seven years later the figure for Chorleywood was a mere 938. Largely wasteland — Roe or Roughwode dates to the 13th century — it had been the least profitable of the church's holdings and, after the Dissolution, fell to different lords. By the 17th century The Cedars was the dominant estate, and the community was ruled by vestry, parish council, and finally urban district council in 1913.

Mills, grazing, charcoal and labouring supported a small community, some of it living in hovels on the commonland, some serving in the great houses — Chorleywood House, Loudwater, The Cedars, and some in the farms that punctuated the hills and valleys. Papermaking flourished for a time, Herbert Ingram of the *Illustrated London News* buying Loudwater Mill in 1848. In an age of literacy, when the *ILN* could sell six figures weekly, Chenies had its school in 1846, and Chorleywood seven years later. There were still poor, so almshouses went up in 1861 and in 1881: Chenies lost theirs in 1888. A year later 'Charley Wood' was a 'hamlet 2½ miles from Rickmansworth Railway Station', and later that year the railway arrived. Times had changed.

The railway brought people, but not all mod. cons. The roads were not surfaced until 1914, and it took until 1922 to get a meeting place — the Memorial Hall, cost £4,000. Diesel, then electrification brought a fast shuttle service to Town, and Metroland became commuter country. In the 1950s Chorleywood had the highest per capita income in the UK.

By 1951 Chorleywood had grown to 4,432 — a fourfold increase in half a century. That year plans were unfurled for doubling the population to 8,700, in 300 acres of new housing — municipal development in Quickley and Berry Lanes, mixed south of the railway, and private sector at Loudwater.

'The shopping facilities in Chorleywood are not good' quoth the county planners, and decreed these should be extended to Shire Lane, and (rather cheekily) over the border in Bucks. Open space? Chorleywood House and the Common boasted 180 acres — that should be enough. Average rate of growth was to range between 50 and 60 houses per annum.

Three years later, Chenies went under the hammer. The 12th Duke died in a shooting accident, and death duties demanded some sacrifice. Chenies was chosen, and four and a half centuries of patronage were finally laid to rest.

The great auction raised £182,000, when Sir Bernard Docker, the golden Daimler tycoon, chaired the winning bidder, Metropolitan Railway Estates Ltd, who only wanted 200 acres near Chalfont, for speculative development. Most of the tenants got their homes at relatively knock-down prices. But the estate was irrevocably broken up, and the 'model village' no longer and nevermore a single entity. Altogether 1,676 acres, 44 homes, seven farms, a pub, 255 acres of woodland, the watercress beds, corrugated cubicled swimming pool on the Chess, and fishing rights were offered.

Great Green Street Farm fetched a respectable £66,000 with its 276 acres; at 131 acres, Newhouse Farm went for £25,000. The cricket ground raised a handsome £1,700 and the allotments, £450. Cottages went for anything from £1,150 for No 4 to £2,700 for the pair at 42 and 3.

Farmer Bill Simpson, who rented Great House Farm, put in a bid of £150,000 to try to keep the village 'in house', but Lord Wimborne soon topped that, and in the end Sir Bernard's men won the day. Some lots were withdrawn, and the final figure was reportedly around £108,000.

In 1974 great upheavals beset the land when, not for the first time, the rulers decreed a change of rules. Chenies found itself a miniscule outlier of Chiltern District Council, and

Chorleywood was subsumed within the mighty Three Rivers. In a strange way, the two communities thus reached back to their roots — river and hill, water and ancient tribe.

Today, Chorleywood has achieved a considerable community image, retained its commonland, and escaped the worst encroachments of urbania. Chenies has crystallised much of its inherent charm around a tidy, if less well-treed green, with a sensitive manorial presence, and the benefit of not being on the main road to anywhere.

The pictures which follow try to catch a short span of years, when Chenies was still a village 'in hand', and Chorleywood yet to become a considerable place.

Front Cover: Green Street provides the link between Chenies and Chorleywood — leading down from the ancient village to what became Chorleywood West, once the railways came. Even today, between cars, just beyond Little Green Street Farm, before the urban rows of Metroland stretch across the horizon, this one-time track retains its tranquillity. (VJ)

In the valley of the Chess, (or Isen — the iron stream) the Romans built at intervals of just under two miles; inevitably, the later Saxons and their Norman successors were equally attracted to this verdant vale. The old church for Flaunden lay between Latimer and Chenies, by the riverside, fell into ruin and is now no more. This is how it looked a hundred years and more ago — with its adjoining cottage. Not far away a spring near Bell Hill fed the watercress beds, which flourished until the 1950s — with daily consignments to Covent Garden. The lowered water table reduced the source, and sewage polluted the cressbeds. (RM)

Mills supplied power to convert grain from the valley fields — and it was the river that made them possible. The Old, Chenies or Dodd's Mill — after John Dodd, who died in 1857 — was on the road to Sarratt. It turned from corn to fulling cloth in the 12th century, then papermaking in the 18th — the area prospered from advanced manufacturing techniques into the following century — and back to corn, until finally it ground cattle feed, until it closed in 1933. The last corn miller was Mr Todd; then Charles Bastin lived and worked there from 1926, sub-tenant to John Henry Boughton, tenant to the Duke. In 1970 Trafford Boughton bought it for £16,500 — his grandfather's aunt was Sarah Dodd. Today it is a private house. (CS)

Today the great god car rules the roads. Yesterday public transport was commonplace — in post-war years eight 'buses plied for hire through Chenies every day — four there and four back. The service started in 1921 — before that the Bedford Arms provided a twice daily horse-drawn station carriage. LEFT: Route 336 from Rickmansworth to Chesham via Chenies took the high road through Chorleywood, detoured through the village, and thence through Chesham to the 'Nash'. For a short time in the early '30s, it took the low road via Latimer, but that never caught on. Rover Buses tried it too for a time. This AEC half-cab was once a familiar sight. The service continues today, albeit less frequently. (CB) RIGHT: The 'country' route, through the Loudwater estate, was appropriately labelled 336A, and this Leyland Cub paused here near Sarrat in 1951. (VJ)

Before the 1914-18 War, motor transport of any kind was sparse, as this four-seater tourer demonstrates in what was, in 1911, called 'Chenies Valley' — the group of Bedford Estate cottages built alongside the river at the foot of Chenies Hill. (CS)

LEFT: In the 1930s, this was one of a pair of Mill cottages, now Mill Farm. The footbridge has gone. High up in the gable is the Bedford coronet and date — 1847. Mrs Rose Maling holds her son Kenneth; beside her, sister Hilda Bastin; David Maling stands on the bridge with cousin John Bastin. (RM) RIGHT: Down by the riverside, His Grace the 11th Duke tries for a pre-war trout, his retainers discreetly observing his prowess with rod and line . . . The trout drastically declined around 1927, but have become a feature of the Chess Valley in recent years. (RM)

The home of the Dowager Duchess Adeline, Woodside (House) was once a boarding school. The Duchess made a habit of giving Christmas gifts to the village children — one year it was a red riding hood for the girls and a red jersey for the boys. When she died, the Forbes sisters came, and then Mrs Wishart and Mrs Stafford Charles. During World War II the Army took over, and now it is divided into four homes. (CS)

The view down Chenies Hill, with Woodside on the right, includes White Hill, the footpath cut out of the chalk bank on the left, published at the turn of the century by Smith Bros of Market Square, Chesham. Today the trees obscure the path, itself somewhat overgrown. Here the butcher's boy drives uphill with his deliveries. (CS)

Up the drive at Woodside, Alf Foote and his wife, Milly, plus their son, Ted, pose in the Duchess's grand tourer, with its acetylene lamps and spare tyre. (RM)

Some of the cottages in the village are Tudor, though the majority are 19th century Rev Lord Russell developments — he was for some six decades a more than benevolent Rector. A. & C. Black's idyllic view c1920 reflects a pastoral past, with its romanticised vista at the top of Chenies Hill, on the edge of the Green. (CS)

In the original schoolhouse (now extended, but still off the Green, near Manor and Church) there were 80 places in 1864. There was an infant school for 40 and a 'school of industry' — for strawplait? The children c1910 numbered around 50, with Headmaster 'Old Tommy' James, middle class mistress Miss Haynes and the infants' Miss Turtle. Most left at 14 to work in service or the fields, and conditions were spartan: the toilets comprised a multi-holer plank across buckets, emptied daily, the contents buried in the school garden. Around 1890, the children posed for the camera — Edward George Cocks was in charge and Mary Ballenger looked after the infants. (RM)

In those early 1900s, little girls were dwarfed by the great Royal oak, allegedly planted by good Queen Bess in Tudor times, to make her local mark on one of her expensive progresses (in 1570), in the field by the Manor House. It is dated to 1570 but some claim an earlier provenance. It survives somewhat stunted, on the Platt. (CS)

Chenies House, by the Church, was home to Algernon Wriothesley Russell in 1887. By 1910 Miss Russell lived there, and then Lady Blandford. Mr Kilby was the butler. The Army took over during World War II and the death watch beetle after that. Post-war, the house was demolished, and a modern home stands on the site today. (CB)

St Michael's Parish Church is 15th century with a 12th century font and other surviving fragments, within 1861 and 1887 restorations. There are several interesting memorials, but its glory is greatly enhanced by the Bedford Chapel, which reflects the Russell connection as the family's final resting place. Coles of Watford published this attractive turn of century view, across Chenies House gardens. (CS)

Chenies Manor c1900: place and manor take their name from the family Chenduit or Cheyne of the 13th century through there are traceable elements to Domesday; the estate was part of Chalfont St Giles at that time. In 1530 the house was rebuilt: Leland reported 'The olde House of the Cheyneis is so translated by my Lorde Russel that litle or nothing of it yn a maner remaynith untranslated . . .' Clearly the first Earl was a modernist. One wing survives. Great House Farm during the 19th and much of the 20th century, it has been lovingly and sensitively restored in recent years, gaining an enviable reputation for its herb garden. (CS)

These young ladies of the village, in their Sunday best, coiffed and carefully gowned, have left this pleasant prospect of the end of last century to posterity, regrettably without their names. (RM)

LEFT: *Near the Manor, planted on the ridge centuries ago, Lady Cheney's Walk was a magnificent avenue of elms — until the Dutch disease decimated them in the '70s. Today they are no more, but a footpath still marks the route they took — from Copse Wood to Walk's Wood and Stony Lane. (CS) RIGHT: Launched in the '20s by Mesdames Wishart and Charles, Chenies Women's Institute was well to the fore on public occasions, as with this display and banner, and these championship chicks, all trayed up and nowhere to go under their wire netting canopy on an ample lap. The Thorleys cap suggests a degree of commercial sponsorship. (RM)*

Joe Bastin of Chenies ploughs a lonely furrow on Old House Farm, Chenies — in fact, nearer Chalfont, by Bell Lane — in the '30s, epitomising the rural life of those days, with its round stacks, two-blade wooden plough and teamed horse-power. (RM)

This 1920s float for some unidentified village affair was mounted on a wooden-wheeled, chain-driven 3-ton truck, with an open cab. The ladies are believed to be from the Chenies WI, and the picture is probably just after the first World War. (RM)

Boy meets girl on bicycle in a vastly different setting before the Great War, when the Green was just that — green. Massed elms, the railed-off well and dirt roads suggest a seclusion and serenity undisturbed by latterday motorcars and tourists. The elms have gone — but replantings lend hope for future generations. The well once boasted a little spring, and a tap which allowed a pool to form. There is still a tap today, and a pump which does not work. There is also brickwork instead of protective wiring. (CS)

Prominent by the Green are Nos 42 and 3 — once separate Tudor cottages, and now combined and modernised with proper regard for their period, as one extremely desirable residence; beyond lie typical Russell cottages, with their gothic chimneys. These buildings typify the way Chenies has adapted its heritage to contemporary life. (CS)

The Chenies Cricket Team, complete with umpire, reserve and coach — and what appears to have been a mascot: the old English sheepdog between the Captain's legs, before World War I. (RM)

The Old Berkeley (later Mills — after Bertram) Coach passes Miss Glenister's home c1910 — a revival of a form of transport that almost certainly never went through the village in the heyday of the turnpikes and stage coach. It made the journey from Wendover to Rickmansworth twice weekly for the first two decades of this century, changing horses at the Bedford Arms. In the 1860s, Thomas Barr, landlord of the Arms, was both blacksmith and carrier as well. Two decades later, William Brown carried goods to Town Monday and Thursday, returning Wednesday and Friday. The Station 'bus called on its way to Rickmansworth from Amersham: depart 8.30 am, return 7 pm — except Sundays. (CS)

The pre-fire Bedford Arms in the 1930s — Thomas Barr ran it 80 years before; Charles Frederick Goodson in the 1880s. It was owned by the Russells until 1954, when it went with the rest of the estate. Fire broke out at 10 am on Christmas Day 1972. 25 staff and 10 guests owed their lives to the quick thinking and courage of manager Tom Blakeway, who was badly burned. Thirty firemen were needed to put out the blaze. (RM)

During World War II, the village fielded its own fire brigade — part time firemen, who included Sam Beeson, Jimmy Atkins, Alf Holloway and George Hearn. (RM)

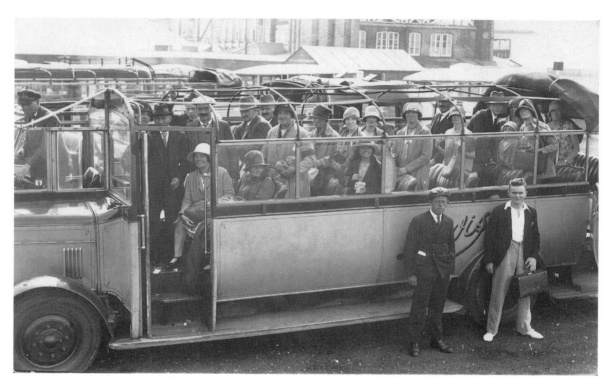

Often, during those halcyon inter-war years, the village took off for charabanc outings. This happy crowd left for Portsmouth in the early '30s. (RM)

The Post Office has had three homes in its time. The second one was in the left-hand cottage of this pair near the Bedford Arms. In 1887 Miss Jane Glenister was postmistress and there were deliveries at 7.45 and 1 and collections at 10.15 and 5.30 — but the money order office was at Chorleywood. Jane and Hannah Glenister were the village linen drapers and grocers too. (CS)

H. W. Wilson was once in charge and ran tea rooms in the third and final Post Office, between the two pubs. Sub Postmistress Miss Phipps kept things going in the sixties, and the facility finally closed in 1975. (CS)

The Old Berkeley Hunt — now part of the Vale of Aylesbury — was kennelled on Chorleywood Common, so it was a short step up Green Street, across the top road and down past the Red Lion to take the hounds for a constitutional. Then as now, they made a traditional subject for an unknown Edwardian photographer. (CS)

Chenies' other, equally popular hostelry, the Red Lion is somewhat overshadowed by the trees in this early 20th century study by Coles of Watford. Cars park now where these little girls took their ease. Older residents remember playing in the road and rushing to see a car — a rare event in the first decade of the century when 'we ran to the gate to see them go by'. (CS)

The Baptist congregation first met in James Newton's house in 1705 and Cheynes Lodge, the home of James Cannon, in 1708. The chapel was established in 1760, and the present building went up in 1779, built by William Davis, steward to the Duke. (RM).

The Baptist Sunday School was well attended, as this forty-plus turnout witnessed c1905, when Rev Fursdon was the minister. (RM)

Chenies Bakery and tea rooms were here, near the main road, on the opposite side to the Rectory — a house now somewhat extended. Mr Salmon baked between the wars. (CS)

J. H. Croft of Church Street, Rickmansworth, took this carefully posed picture for posterity. In the bath chair was Rector Rev Shand's wife, and pushing it was Annie Ayres (then Bastin). The picture dates to c1910. The bath chair was often used by children at Sunday School treats, to race around the Rectory garden. (RM)

This pleasant prospect has not essentially changed since this c1900 picture was taken of the 'approach to village', as photographer Coles described it. (CS)

LEFT: Mrs Puddephatt stands proudly before No 9, New Cottages in what looks like a summer shot. There are irises in a splendid glazed-ware pot in the window, and on the front wall of this house, near the main road, is the Bedford coronet and the date of the building — 1867. (RM) RIGHT: This charming study of two sisters and pony takes us down towards Chorleywood, by way of Green Street, in the long hot summers of those far-off Edwardian days. (CS)

Across the road from Chenies, there was once a small hamlet with almshouses, a meeting house for the Congregationalists (formed 1760 under pastor Bennet) in a commodious outbuilding by one of several cottages, and two farms. The farmhouse remains in one case, the farm in the other, alongside Green Street, where these were the Countess of Warwick's almshouses, founded 1603 — 10 tenements of two rooms each. In 1830 there were 72 people there, 68 of them in rooms meant for six. They were mostly from Northaw and Wotton, whence came the endowment funds. The Trust was thrown into Chancery, resolved in 1887, when the building and its endowment lands were sold for £650. The Duke paid another £850 against his repair liability, and Chenies got £900 6s to invest, for five pensioners, two of them men. Having bought it, the Duke wanted to turn it into cottages but, piqued by abusive letters, he pulled it down instead — in 1888. This is how it looked in 1847. (CB)

Green Street took the would-be rail traveller from Chenies down the hill, to Chorleywood West — green fields when the railway came in 1889 — looking east across what is now Blacketts Wood Drive. Tracy's Stores is in the middle ground by the railway arch, Old Farm to its right, and behind that, on the skyline, the Hotel. (VJ)

By 1936 the railway embankment had acquired a clothing of trees, and development had filled in some of the gaps in the burgeoning Hertfordshire settlement, but not on the Buckinghamshire side. The Hotel is on the extreme right, Old Farm in the left foreground, and Tracy's on the extreme left. (CB)

In this early 20th century close-up, taken from two separate pictures, Tracy's is on the right, proclaiming the post office and the public telephone, and Old Farm on the left, offering hunters and hacks for hire, and advertising tea gardens. Lower Road is marked by the corner lamp post. The South Road Baptists also advertised their meetings and divine worship every Sunday. C. Jones ran Old Farm, whose phone number was 10. (VJ)

South Road presented a pretty rough texture to the horsed traffic of the early 20th century. It also provided the boundary between the two counties, and marked the edge of Chorleywood West. Here building is beginning on the Bucks side, and shops are developing along Lower Road, C. F. Pain Ltd, chemist, succeeding Goss on the corner site, where before was only garden. (CB)

Tracy's opened for business in 1904, the only shop in Chorleywood West, providing postal services as well, hard by the railway arch at the foot of Shire Hill. While the other staff posed outside, 'Babs' wrote this card inside, around 1905. Only 15 years previously, the year after the railway was extended to Chorleywood, there were no shops listed at all in local directories. (VJ)

Tracy's moved by 1910, and expanded into butchery, and other shops like Wilson's had joined them in Colleyland. Tracy's demonstrated loyalty to the Crown with the letters ER on their brickwork, but took the letters down, presumably on the King's death — the outline is just visible in this picture, with the store's delivery van, gaslighting and well-stocked windows bespeaking growing prosperity for the new settlement. (VJ)

The view back down Shire Lane in Edwardian days once more demonstrates the sharp divide the aptly named Hill provided between the two counties, and the open fields, undeveloped, beyond the railway line. Tracy's is on the left, a lonely Buckinghamshire outpost. (VJ)

The children of Heronsfield School in Shire Lane in the late 1940s dress up as fairies, complete with Pan's pipes — for the school summer event. (VJ)

Lower Road, when war broke out in 1914, looked somewhat less trafficked and shopped than it does today. Young's Stores provided this view, the ironmongery in the corner building on the right, Ryders on the opposite corner, and the cottage (centre) known as Maystone, after its builder, Mr Stone — he developed Chorleywood Bottom too. (VJ)

LEFT: The Baptist Chapel, originally built as a church hall, but pressed into use for worship because a church was never built, was up Hillside Road — the building survives. (VJ) RIGHT: The Guest House was one of a run of detached villas along Station Road — known as Berks Hill, after the Berkhamsted Poor Estate: land originally bought to endow the poor of that town. The Guest House has not survived, but the building has — as a private home. (VJ)

ABOVE: Around 1904, Green Street was a quiet, deserted path, newly fenced, and gaslit. (VJ) BELOW: A goods train pulls slowly through 'Chorley Wood and Chenies Station', between the wars, the Hotel to the right. (VJ)

Chorleywood Hotel, now the Sportsman, was newly built in the 1890s — by 1900 the bank on the left had acquired some 'temporary' shop premises. (HCL)

The shops stayed — Achille Serre, Edlin, (Robinson), the A.I. Boot Depot (Dimmock), Coutts Bank, Swannell and Sly, and Darvell's coal merchant. Clearly Station Approach was also a favourite venue for playing with your hoop.
(VJ)

Common Road in about 1910, winds up from the 'new' settlement, alongside the Common itself, the Golf Club on the left. The iron shed was once the railway navvies' canteen, then Rose's Tea Rooms. (HCL)

Riding to hounds was a serious business in 1911, with ladies side-saddled, Eton collar and cloak for the younger rider, fawn Derbies and top hats de rigeur, and hunt servants properly liveried. The kennel man wore the regulation white coat, at the Chorleywood Kennels of the Old Berkeley Hunt. (VJ)

It was the Golf Club roller that ran out of control, and demolished the right hand end of the kennels complex, when it ran off the edge of the green after some children set it off by accident. Amy Tofield was one of them. The Master's house was added on the left. (VJ)

At the junction of Common Road and the main road to Rickmansworth and Watford, two ponds provided a landmark and a favourite spot for recreation, here c1905. The Lodge to Chorleywood House was over the road. (VJ)

Chorleywood House, once the property of Lady Monica Ela Sackville Russell, the Duke of Bedford's sister, became the offices of the Urban District Council and later, of Three Rivers Council; its future is uncertain — conversion to flats is mooted. (VJ)

One of the more prolific postcard publishers before the first World War was F. Evans, hairdresser of Chorley Wood (sic). His study of Christ Church is one of the best — before trees obscured this view, after 1906. The original chapel of ease was built in 1845 and rebuilt in 1870. The School next door was founded in 1853. (VJ)

The Old Shepherd was run between the wars by Mr Sills, whose son Len poses in front of the pub in this 1920s study.
(VJ)

On the corner of Solesbridge Lane and the A404, grocer J. Pullen ran Chorleywood Post Office — hence the soubriquet 'Post Office Corner', in this early 20th century picture. At the top of Solesbridge Lane children spent many happy hours watching the blacksmith at work in the late '30s.

The Gate Inn, a favourite watering hole for generations of passers-by as well as for residents, presented a peaceful view of today's heavily trafficked route from town to country, with Weller's Entire to quench your thirst, a hack for hire, or a trap to take you home, if your hand was a little too unsteady for the reins. (VJ)

Down the Lane, the old Primitive Methodist Chapel was demolished 1895. Once the Quakers met there. Mrs Humphrey poses in front of a demonstrably primitive chapel, broom to the fore. (HCL)

LEFT: *Tollgate House took its name from the old turnpike keeper's cottage, and became the home of renowned actor-manager of the St James Theatre, (Sir) George Alexander, seen RIGHT: with Irene Vanbrugh in 'His House in Order'. He built Lutyens' Court in 1911, died in 1918, and was the first to stage Wilde's 'The Importance of Being Ernest', 'Lady Windermere's Fan' and 'The Second Mrs Tanqueray'. The Almshouses nearby were built by the Gilliats. (VJ)*

The White Horse, a Salter's house, earlier this century, is allegedly Chorleywood's oldest inn, on the Gout Road.
(HCL)

Off Dog Kennel Lane, across the Common, squatters built, as was so often the case, on commonland — here at Apple Tree Dell. Artichoke and Cherry Tree Dells were similarly settled. It all looks so idyllic in 1905 but, on closer inspection, life was fairly primitive, with water butt and night soil bucket outside the door. Henry Wood lived at Apple Tree Farm. (VJ)

It is unnecessary to be a 'political' animal to recognise the sharp difference between a squatter's hovel on the commonland and The Cedars, a 17th century estate, rebuilt 1865, in 1917 Chorleywood College for the Blind, itself now removed in July 1987 to Worcestershire. The house was built by Mr Gilliat. (VJ)

The blind girls tended the garden at the Cedars — under supervision, in this early 20th century shot; on the right, fingertip control deploys a rose support. (VJ)

Not far from the big house were Cedars Cottages — another 'constructive' use of commonland, where sheep might safely graze, and hay be stacked, little girls confer in secret, and cottagers lean over their (quite posh) metal railings to examine a neighbour's baby in its pram, proud parents pausing for their admiration, the domestic linen flapping in the breeze behind. After World War I, Irish leader Michael Collins met Government men to settle the terms of the Irish Treaty, in a cottage on the Common. (VJ)

There was an Auxiliary Hospital in Chorleywood during the Great War of 1914-18. R. Frier took this picture of what look like perfectly fit soldiers, undeniably at Chorleywood, and with a gun carriage. Their hat badges look suspiciously like those of the Royal Artillery. Perhaps there were exercises on the Common? (VJ)

When the railway navvies were rehoused in something more permanent, the Black Horse replaced the Finch's Arms, near their hovels — the original pub was once Constable's Cottage, an alehouse in its parlour, and later became the Winchelsea Arms, before its relocation, forced through by the lady at the Cedars, who objected to a pub on her doorstep. (HCL)

In Chorleywood Bottom, Younger's Retreat provided a favourite day excursion destination in the Edwardian era. Tea was 6d a go and there were pony rides, swings and what looks like a loud hailer — presumably to marshall the children when it was time to go home. (VJ)

Off Stag Lane, King's Farm exposes its Tudor ancestry, and recalls the Pennsylvania and Quaker connection; here William Penn married his Gulielma Springett in 1672. (CB)

The Swillet, where records state there was a natural 'swill', as water carved a bowl out of the gravel, boasted shopkeeper J. A. Snook and Blackett's Stores in Edwardian days. In 1853, it was aptly named — with no less than three beer retailers. (VJ)

Heronsgate or Herringsgate in 1846 comprised 103 acres of neglected land. Wm Hunt gladly sold 'Herringers' for £2,344 to idealist Feargus O'Connor's Chartist Land Co. O'Connor built houses for a workers' utopia, O'Connorville, where temperance reigned, and men would go back to Mother Earth. The experiment failed. The Old Farm House looked a bit the worse for wear by the early 20th century. (VJ)

The topers had the last laugh on poor O'Connor. Just across the border of his utopia, they built this tavern — and aptly dubbed it Land of Liberty. Thus are the dreams of reformers brought down to earth. (VJ)

Gin may have been mother's ruin, and beer the last resort of the working man, but water is what created Chorleywood, long before the railway came, and water was the foundation of Isenhampstead Chenduit too. Even today, the serenity of the stream we call the Chess is still to be seen in the valley — here between Chenies and Chorleywood in April 1907.
(CS)

Index to Illustrations